Hallelujah Time!

Poems by
John L. Stanizzi

ISBN: 978-0-9908413-4-0

Printed in the United States of America

Back Cover photo: David Oliver
Cover Designed by: Christopher Reilley

Also by John L. Stanizzi:

Windows
Sleepwalking: Poems
Ecstasy Among Ghosts
Dance Against the Wall
After the Bell

Big Table Publishing Company
Boston, MA bigtablepublishing.com

Acknowledgements

I would like to express my gratitude to Robin Stratton, Bessy Reyna, Susan Holmes, David Ferry, Kwame Dawes, Jon Andersen, Rennie McQuilkin, and Cedella Marley. I am also grateful for the light of Rastafari. Blessed love.

Some of the poems in *Hallelujah Time!* appeared previously in the following magazines:

"Get Up, Stand Up" – *Solo Novu: 122 Days*
"Guiltiness", "Natural Mystic", "I Shot the Sheriff "– *Third Wednesday*
"Hallelujah Time!" – *Emerge Literary Journal*
"Small Axe" –*burning bush (Dublin, Ireland)*
"Pass it On" – *Redheaded Stepchild*
"The Heathen", "So Much Trouble in the World" – *Shapes*
"Exodus" – *Red River Review*
"One Foundation" – *Rattle*
"Burnin' and Lootin'" – *Poetry Quarterly*
"Waiting in Vain" – *Connecticut River Review*
"Turn Your Lights Down Low" – *Long River Run*
"Three Little Birds", "Duppy Conquerer" – *Gap Toothed Madness*

For Carol, for my children, for my mother,
and as always, for Clem

"In a room where people unanimously maintain a conspiracy of silence, one word of truth sounds like a pistol shot."
~Czesław Miłosz

Contents

Burnin'
(1974)

Get Up, Stand Up

Jesus saith unto him, Rise, take up thy bed, and walk.
~ John 5:8

Before the love-in, the sit-down, or the uprising,
you will notice,
from the vast valley of groundless sleep,
that the light has begun to shift,
to move imperceptibly across the dark room
in widening stripes of bright light,
and you may be tempted to turn over,
curl up, and resist the sunrise.

Before you Save the Children,
Feed the Homeless
or chant down the Tea Party,
you must confront
that ascending cocktail of dust,
the pollen and hair,
paper and fibers,
minerals and soil,
the burnt out meteors
and human cells
that waft in lengthening cones of sunlight.

You'll have to acknowledge the tonnage of your legs,
the pain and weakness,
the monumental focus necessary to move them
and feel the cool floor solid beneath your feet.

Get up.

Stand up into that massive reach of light
and move past the maple's marbled disease,
the pond wimpling the trees and the sky,
and farther,
touching the entire landscape at once,
beyond the unwrapped birches,
into the far hills rolling over themselves,
devouring the air deeply,
out beyond the inconsequential words
spoken under low yellow lights,
and farther still,
out to where listening
is the prayer spiriting your fears,
while behind you always
the great voice
sounds its trumpet.

Hallelujah Time!

Let everything that has breath praise the Lord. Praise you the Lord.
~ Psalms 150:6
~ For my granddaughter, Raelle Lynne Stanizzi, 21 months old

There are eleven deer standing on the ridge,
but you catch a glimpse only by mistake;
the setting sun erases their silhouettes.
First they're deer then they're something less,
something like those hidden object games,
until they're only what you *thought* you saw,
a little obscurity that stays with you
as an Indian Summer breeze lifts and whispers
through the sieve of December trees along the hill,
a translation from one mysterious language to
another. It speaks of living on borrowed time
and of a hallelujah of deer appearing there
on the crest of a hill that reaches down to where
Raelle, in her tiny chilly body, plays,
but stops when she sees me, stops and runs to me,
runs to *me*, leaving one imagined privacy
for another – her sense of what I am to her –
recognizing in me something capable of love.
How mystical, this little winter drama,
so blessed that for a moment I think I can smell
Spring in the winter air, its scent of rain.

I Shot the Sheriff

...thou knowest not whether shall prosper, either this or that,
or whether they both shall be alike good.
~ Ecclesiastes 11:6

I didn't do it, Billy wept, bouncing
up and down on the edge of the hard wood chair,
and punching his finger at me as I came in.
He did! He did! Johnnie wrote the word!
He was the 3rd grade vandal who had defaced the book
room with a magic marker that I'd stolen
from Sister Maria Richard's gray metal desk.
But he wasn't telling the truth, and I was shocked.
It was true that I had removed a couple of books
from the shelf, but I didn't do the graffiti;
it was Billy who quickly scrawled the word *Ass*
on the wall before I replaced the books
to hide the word, immediately feeling remorse.
I've never forgotten the image of him selling me out
through his fear and tears, crying and calling my name.
Oh, the lessons learned that afternoon.
　　　　I took the books down,
　　　　But I didn't tag the wall that day.

When we were only kids, 13 or so,
I'd sneak out of my room at 2 a.m.,
shift my father's battered van to neutral,
roll down the drive and start it on the run.
Mark would sneak out and wait for me in the shadows
of the hedges out in front of his house.
Then we'd drive the length of Old Main Street,

and every time we passed the sign that read
Speed Is Checked By Radar, I would yell
Fuck the radar, and drop it into low;
the van would lurch and growl and we would laugh.
This was a coming of age, a rite of passage
whose adolescent light was fading out,
and though we couldn't comprehend the truth,
Old Main was getting smaller and we were moving
farther and farther away from innocence.
        I'd sneak the van out,
        But I never took the Dodge Coronet.

It seems the older I get, the more Viet Nam
tries to pry its way into the things I write,
the words I say. And yet, if truth be told,
my tendency these days is to not resist,
but rather let those thoughts of cowardice
and lies and violent death and anger born
of confusion so profound it covered me–
let them make their way back to the front,
shabby old veterans of my imagination,
and live where the seasons' diversities bevel the past,
making things seem much smoother than they are.
Like now; the cold has come and the moon is out,
a little hole too small to push your head through, but
big enough to remind you of the light
that is beyond our capacity to comprehend;
there it is, pressing against the dark.
        I shot at targets
        But I never killed a human being.

This is one of those poems that isn't sure
what it's trying to say. Or maybe it's me.
Either way, there's self-indulgence here,
an attempt to justify even those times
when what occurred was well beyond my means
to challenge it; it's the way it was.
But the way it was is endearing in a way
that is a comfort; the years gone by, the body
giving in, and yet what's *wild* takes on
a meaning I can actually pray about.
The birds were clay but now they're jittery visitors
who come in droves to my feeders every day,
and the deer beneath the apple tree and moon
still nibble the frozen apples on the ground;
these are what I'm drawn to now because
this is the kind of feral you cannot touch.
I postured as *bad*
But I really was a foolish child.

These days I'm riding the spiral come round,
and while it seems that everything is hurtling
forward much faster now, it's all the same;
a part of me completely understands.
It's all about perception and urgency,
and in whatever moments I'm allowed
to take another breath and look around,
I'll praise the silence, because the silence was
the voice that spoke of Babylon and greed,
the voice that showed me where the grandeur is,

in the trust that smolders in my children's eyes,
the spider web created over night,
a magnified gem in the light of the rising sun,
the baby catfish, smaller than my pinkie,
that rest in the mud at the bottom of the frozen pond,
and the billion mysteries I will never comprehend.
I'm inconsistent
But tomorrow I'll rethink it all.

Burnin' And Lootin'

Through thee will we push down our enemies:
through thy name will we tread them under that rise up against us.
~ Psalms 44:5

(For my son, Jonathan, after an incident that occurred when he was 12)

One autumn night they met down by
The factory bleak and hollow,
The stars above the shattered glass
Were the lights that they would follow.

They didn't dare to go inside
Where shadows might have faces,
And bony arms might hold them there –
Imagination races.

No, they preferred the parking lot
Behind the shabby shop,
The battered asphalt splayed by weeds
Back where the moonlight dropped.

Halloween was in the air,
Cool and mischievous;
They snuck behind the shadows, how
They were villainous;

With BB guns and no real plan,
They hustled around the back,
And opened fire excitedly
On the windows that were cracked.

And one could hear the falling glass
As voices off the sea
Present themselves to distant ears
As clear as they can be.

And so the cops were summoned there
To where the shots were fired,
To drop the hammer on these offenders
And the trouble they inspired.

Eight cruisers poured into the lot –
Tires and sirens wail –
Suffusing the villains with their lights
Against the building's shale.

And when the cops could see their eyes,
And knew that these were kids,
You might have thought that they'd back off,
Take another tack instead.

They might have harkened back to their
Own adolescent days,
And the allure of a vacant plant
In the evening's haze,

Its windows begging to be smashed;
There's little harm in this
Boyish act, this rite of passage,
this childish carelessness.

But they came in brutal uniforms;
One knelt on a neck –
Move a muscle and you're dead!
Brandishing a Glock.

And I wonder *Was it really worth it?*
This vicious show of strife,
To treat these kids like criminals,
So they'd hate you all their lives.

Put It On

Now Israel loved Joseph more than all his children, because he was the son of his old age: and he made him a coat of many colours.
~ Genesis 37:3

i *Feel them spirit*

Depending on your mood, the weather, the headlines,
it might be the veery in harmony with itself,
singing of the silent fleeting fusion of night
and day; it might be the flat, grassy fields
along the river, the bull, belly deep
in muck, and eyeing you with what it seems
is an attitude that says *just keep on paddling,*
and the throaty train whistle sounds above the rumble
of iron wheels on track, another harmony –
the wail of song above our deep concerns;
the robe of glory is sewn with just such things,
and it fits perfectly over your skin and bones,
the world emblazoned on the lengthy sleeves,
the lining made of every evening sky.

ii *I'm not boasting*

The clay road to the dirty river wound
a thousand miles of hot and dusty earth
that billowed from beneath our rattling bikes,
and the fields of alfalfa rounded off along
the horizon, as the river scrolled slowly by,
warm and filthy, with a stench that others smelled,
though we could not, and then there was a path
under heavy oaks that led us to the water,
and it was cool and the iridescent leaves

of the skunk cabbage gave a little heat to the flies
that had pollinated the dark flowers that hid beneath
the rotting leaves and melting snow; our engines,
clothespins holding baseball cards to spokes,
roared out the illusion that we were wise,
though we were only 10 and rushing things,
and when we finally got to the riverbank,
the tips of Hartford gleamed on the other side,
and I flipped my oily jackknife open and closed,
while Quanito lit a cigar as long as a pencil
and nearly big around as his balled up fist.

iii *I'm gonna put it on*

the pinball machine at the 10 Pin Bowling Alley
girls curled around singing neon lights
nine dimes in a line and all mine
though I would rarely spend a single one
the machine's front legs lifted onto my sneaks
the silver ball barely rolling now
and bulky sweaters and "you wanna take it outside?"
and a flashlight beam in the back seat of my car
breathy breathing in the winter parking lot
gumball cop cars 96 Tears of static
and booby traps and numbers in my head
and Christmas tree cadavers here and there
and breaking boards with the side of my hand to prove
that I could live through unimaginable fear
Cool Jerk sucker punch in The Land of 1000 Dances
torsion sunrises helical afternoons
and angry voices echoing off bathroom stalls
and trains leaving sadness at the station
and on the trains contagion in the air

spreading lies about democracy
and what it means and costs to be a man
and though the sunlight always reaches through the spaces
between the leaves and branches of the elm
the massive ambush happens just the same
until the day that I became aware
that those simple good-byes I said in '68
would hang forever in the thinning air

Small Axe

Whoso causeth the righteous to go astray in an evil way,
he shall fall himself into his own pit…
~ Proverbs 28:10

moon set dawn
when I heard those words
the first time

weapons of mass destruction
imminent and threatening

the morning's
blessings beaten by
arrogance

and everything became a
metaphor for dementia

Jesus had
become fictional
the big lie

my father's brain was shattered
but he would force the pieces

John McCain
World War II hero
was his man

he would end this war right now
one dropped bomb to clean up house

a message
to the world about
U.S.A.!

silver and gray rain hit the
windshield – the sound of running –

fleeing a
bully or gunfire –
maybe both

grainy satellite photos
tiny gray objects circled

this is the
way the brain must look
unfocused

grainy bits of memory
in a field of gray chaos

dialogue?
out of context words?
this is proof?

in the end Elektra knew
that she had not gained a thing

the black dawn
was deepened by clouds
haughtiness

the wind banged against our homes –
a sound of desperation

no measure
of compliance would
be enough

what chilling egotism
to forget the taste of fear

to shrug off
the rising voices
with a smirk

to give an ultimatum
you're either with us or them

missiles filled
the air that first day
of springtime

and it needed to be named
a pro-wrestling kind of phrase

to erase
the line between truth
and fiction

Showdown with Saddam: Target Iraq.
Smackdown! Game of Thrones!

half-mast flags
and hero ghosts rose
from the bush

liberation and freedom
a lexicon for the blind

the thumbnail
of the moon was bruised
behind clouds

a photographer of war
took close up shots of the dead

if we saw
what war does close up
we might stop

propaganda custom made
to be acted on a ship

we waxed 'em
mission accomplished
haji dead

there are no large solutions
truths are momentary things

and sadly
flags were raised half staff
in the rain

optimistic confidence
the General's abstraction

casket rows
draped with stars and stripes
disappeared

as if we weren't aware that
illusion is illusion

the crocus
pushed up through the snow
tiny prayers

not some shady sleight of hand
that everyone knew was fixed

they were there
actual flowers
air of spring

bittersweet crept through the heart
of everything that could grow

and this too
would become the past
way back there

setting at O-dark-thirty
too late to begin again

too early
to quit though 10 years
have gone by

10 years watching my father
erasing his own body

10 years of
telling myself that
every thought

is a thing to be recalled
the lies the bombs the coffins

even the
aphasia with its
empathy

Pass It On

Therefore whatsoever ye have spoken in darkness shall be heard in the light...
~ Luke 12:3

An hour after my father died, my mother
asked me if I knew what I had said,
and I answered quickly, trying to give the impression
that I understood, that I was in control.

The late summer dusk that filled the room
touched everything with a gauzy yellow light,
a balm that comforted and eased the pain
of that long last exhalation of relief.

When his last breath came it stilled his trembling,
and what I heard as I sat there by his bed
was the unmistakable sigh of liberation,
a simple *ahhh* that seemed to say *Thank God.*

I told my mother his passing was a gift
that had taken away his anguish and his hurt.
But a year has passed and I've had time to think
about what I would call our last exchange;

I was murmuring words of reassurance
through the thickness of the morphine drip,
and then the light in the room began to shift,
to soften to a comforting shade of yellow.

And that was when he spoke in the language of
the dying, and I took that final sound
into myself, and spoke it in translation;
Thank God I breathed into the darkening room,
a whispered bliss, the suffering left to us.

Duppy Conquerer

For we wrestle not against flesh and blood, but against principalities,
against powers, against the rulers of the darkness of this world,
against spiritual wickedness in high places.
~Ephesians 6:12

1

Hot-bug days along the Connecticut River
marking the start of the end of another summer,
a monotone reminder that this shall pass,
as bloated suckers slowly glided by,
and whole trees still sheathed with all their leaves,
torn from somewhere, drifted by us there,
and logs so water-drenched they barely floated,
and the occasional body we'd hear about on the news,
tokens of the mystery we'd deflect.

We invent myths for the purpose of scaring ourselves,
and other myths to overcome those fears;
it seems to me a way we have of coping
with all we know about the way things end,
which isn't very much, I'll grant you that,
but these creations occupy our time,
provide a legacy and a future too,
so pour them out without moderation,
into the trees feeling silently for the air,
and to the birds' elegant punctuation.
Pour them out into the summer garden
bursting with lessons about the quickness of time,
and pour them out to give us the impression
that we can comprehend the dead who live
within in our hearts, still murmuring something there,
though it may be we're talking to ourselves.

2

And aren't we aiders and abettors as we embrace
the things that we can't see; we search for them,
their absence the very thing that gives us fright,
and we give voice to the shadowy corners and hollows
beneath our beds as well as to the clothes
limp on hangers, a queue of emaciated ghosts
waiting for us to open the closet door
and allow their boneless, headless reticence
to kindle in our minds their craftiness
as we imagine their whispered plan of action.

They're everywhere, so many trapped in the vacuum
between mysteries; there's barely enough room to breathe.
And some revel in stirring things up – knocking
over a lamp, opening a door we want closed,
staying up at all hours disturbing our sleep,
and troubling the air in the room into a chill.

3

I saw one once, a little jumby head
resting on the valance in my room
one late August night in '59,
not much larger than an a nectarine,
and just as bald and solid, this tiny head.
I tried to blink it away but it wouldn't go,
this wrinkly little noggin in my room.

I was sure that when I closed the distance
between us he would vanish into the dream
from which he came and I would return to sleep,
comforted by the being taken away,
so I got out of bed and was not afraid;

I walked toward the little hairless head
perched up on the valance in the dark,
and stared into his old and tiny eyes,
which stared right back at me. And we didn't speak.

And he didn't vanish either, did not return
to those quiet, crooked streets where dreams emerge.
He just looked at me as though he were
about to ask a question, though he was silent.
And after a moment, when I knew that he was real,
I turned from him and got back into bed.

4

In my room that night in 1959,
we stood together face to face, alone,
that little, wizened vestige of a man
as real as the as bloated suckers or trees,
and more real than the bodies from the news;
those we only learned of second-hand.
And me, a child, but one who knew the difference
between the truth and the things that I made up.

And even now, with all the years gone by,
I understand that there are tales we tell,
legends that we know, within ourselves,
based on nothing but our will to grasp
the things that we will never understand.

But he was there that night and watching me,
a look of curiosity on his face,
a silent exchange that went beyond the gift
of comprehension or the realm of words,
a rendezvous whose memory is mine,
and which I understand as mystery.

One Foundation

For other foundation can no man lay than that is laid, which is Jesus Christ.

~ 1 Corinthians 3:11

(Triolet for Carol)

So many things that still feel new
are old, and that's the way it goes.
This is what always happens to
so many things that still feel new.

I think of how I have loved you
all these years, and that just shows
so many things that still feel new
feel new because of the life we chose.

Rastaman Chant

...with violence shall that great city Babylon be thrown down,
and shall be found no more at all.
~ Revelation 18:21

thunder

Thunderstruck by chance in the hoard of Spag's,
Spag's mentality drove me to the record bin,
where I hoped for the *Dark Side of the Moon*,
or *Quardrophenia* or *Houses of the Holy;*
I was *Aladdin Sane* and treasure hunting.

What I found was *Caravan* by *Caravan,*
and *East of Eden's Mercator Projected*,
and for 99 cents, the price scrawled
across the album cover in black marker,
an album that looked like barn wood with the words
Burnin' and *The Wailers* smoking still,
but there was no *Thick as a Brick* or *Fragile.*

I'll admit, I'd never seen a joint so big,
and that was the extent of my compulsion;
I didn't know a thing about the music,
the players, or who Ras Tafari was.
But I laid down my buck, and without a bag, I left
with *Burnin'* and my free tomato plants.

When I got home I put the record on,
and got down on the floor to give a listen.
What happened next... it's hard for me to say.
Two drum rolls, hard and sharp, and then one beat,
a wah-wah, bass, and an emphatic mantra...
Get up, stand up, rim shots on the globe.
thunder struck by chants, and me, rolled out.

funde

It was true – there were no bags at Spag's;
but so what, with a promise of coffee good as gold
and savings that were just *Spagtacular!*

All you needed was a short stack of cash,
and the sense to know you'd see the unexpected;
after all, shopping here was an *adventure.*
But a *religious experience?* Let's be serious.
Converse All-Stars, seedlings, tee shirts, Ban,
and stuff you never even knew you needed –
a horse's head and mane attached to a stick,
a bottle of Bayer with a thousand pills inside,
bathrobes, slippers, grapefruits, 2-wheel bikes,
and toilet brushes for 29 cents piled high
atop a grandfather clock that cost two grand –
remarkable for sure, but not religious.

The bridge from Worcester to Shrewsbury led straight onto
a raggy road that scored the shores of Long Pond
and then kept going past the dead-end streets,
the junkyards of divorce, the crowded malls
of raising children, the battered slums of drugs,
all the wrong turns, the doubling back,
grasping at the things I didn't believe,
believing in things I simply couldn't grasp.

And all the while the funde kept the beat,
a steady rock in lockstep with my heart,
from those first clean turnings of the vinyl on
that little Crosley by the fireplace,
to now.

For all I know my heart had stopped
that day in Worcester, funde taking over,
powering this aging engine until that day
when my work is over and I'll fly
away home...

akete

There was
a trilogy of texts then,
"bibles"
I'd carry

in my right back pocket, and
quote,
quote,
quote,
to anyone
who would listen,

to anyone who wouldn't.

We live
on top
of a crumbling world.

Anais Nin told me this,

though I already knew
that the world was crumbling
spectacular and fiery.

Repeat:

We live on top of a
crumbling world.

The home on the hill,
the pond in the yard,
the mountains reaching
all the way to Munson,
the window
that looks out
on dawn steam

lifting from the Willimantic,
cloud banks filtering sun,
and words,
sometimes my own,

mostly borrowed.

Repeat:

We live on top of a
crumbling world.

It must have been a search for spirit,
that manic, tumbling down year
after year.
That must have been my intent,
though I didn't know it then,
didn't know much then,

or now.

Anais repeating to me quietly,
over and over
that it's crumbling,

and all the while the *Pope Smasher,*
Vatican Basher
Popped and riffed,
rim shots,
bruised knuckles,
fire,
fire,
and more fire.

I was 23 and lost when the music began,
something happening within in spite of me,
something fueling my vexation with iniquity,
something as baffling now as it ever was.

II - Exodus
(1977)

Natural Mystic

...for the trumpet shall sound, and the dead shall be raised...
~ I Corinthians 15-52

She sits on my father's Barcalounger
on his imaginary lap
and speaks to him,
thanking him for visiting today.

She tells him all the places she's seen him,
in the small plane in the July sky,
in the hummingbird she has waited days for,
in the squirrel she says looks empathetically at her.

He's been dead a year now,
but my mother tells me she saw my father
plain as day in a license plate, J O N,
and in the butterfly flitting about the bird bath.

She sits on his lap,
hugging his triangular American flag,
tells him she saw him,
that she'll look for him again tomorrow,

that she'll know when she sees the white van,
the shooting star,
the sunflower seedling in the geranium pot,
the moth clinging to the screen,

that it's him,
he's there,
he'll always be there,
she doesn't have to worry.

So Much Things To Say

…Pilate took water, and washed his hands before the multitude, saying,
"I am innocent of the blood of this just person: see ye to it."
~ Matthew 27:21-24

I.

I thought I'd write a dramatic monologue
where I'd profess to comprehend this league

of men who dared to stare injustice down.
One by one, I'd take their voices on,

and posture as if I had some great insight
into the crushing discrimination they would fight,

II.

as if I could feel, even dimly, what Christ
had witnessed when the Roman soldiers diced

for his humble robe because it was clean,
after the miracles, the denial, and that scene

in Gethsemane when, full of doubt,
He asked about the chances of getting out

of this human mess He was entangled in;
but the question was rhetorical, and when

the nails were driven through His hands He must
have been so disappointed in the trust

that was betrayed that He'd never show His face
again; he'd leave them wondering, this foolish race

of human beings who seem to take in hate
the way they breathe;

III

and Marcus Garvey's fate

was also driven with divine intent.
One God! One Aim! One Destiny! he'd chant.

But in East St. Louis the riots would unwind
one of the bloodiest outrages against mankind.

And the Black Star Line would sail into the gale
of bigotry that howled its vile wail

of rage and guns; George Tyler's one-man raid
nearly succeeded, but Marcus was not waylaid;

like Bob so many years later, he wouldn't be stopped
by bullets, those exclamation points that ached.

III

And out of the ghetto of Stony Gut, St. Thomas,
Paul Bogle would emerge when the promise

of slavery's death was manifest in taxes,
and injustices bludgeoned the people, brutal axes

pounding on Morant Bay, though Governor Eyre
would claim there was no reason for their ire,

they had no right to speak. And so they marched
to the Court House at the Bay, and charged

the local powers with racism and oppression,
hot machetes, sticks, and their mission,

but the Custos called on their volunteer militia;
shots were fired, fires were set, these comitia

raged until the revolution died
in flogging, flames, and gunfire; they were mired

in the bloody venom of violence and ignorancy
that ended in death and the *Eyre Controversy*.

IV

So what is there that I can possibly say,
who never rose to greatness from St. Ann's Bay,

or bled upon a low tau on a hill,
or after being throttled with a thrill,

was hung in the burned out court, a spectacle,
a lesson in truth that is despicable?
These are blessed lives, lives ineffable.

Guiltiness

It is vain for you…to eat the bread of sorrows…
Woe to the downpressors…
~ Psalms 127:2
(For Joann)

Like so many things we incapable of forgetting,
this came out of nowhere,
this diagnosis of squamous cell pharyngeal cancer,
which sounded, over the phone, like *squeamish,*
and that made perfect sense to me.

The doctor said
he wasn't going to sugar coat it.
When you asked about your chances
for survival.
he said *Slim,*
a one-word lightning-strike, tornado
earthquake, tsunami, death-rattle,
your children's faces floating in and out
of the wreckage.

But then the battalion of your humor struck
with laughter and jokes,
as your plan unfolded,
everyone around you feeling less fear.

This was how you'd fight,
I thought,
recalling all the times
I'd underestimated you.

You'd go to *Lakeview* for lunch,
sit on the deck overlooking the water
and watch the ducks forage around the dock.

Then you'd go to *Hair Trendz*
to cut off all your hair;
you weren't going to hang around until you woke up
surrounded by long
locks of blond,
that mess;
you'd make the first move.

After that you'd stop at our house
for a couple of cold Coronas,
explaining that since chemo
was starting on Monday
you needed to do a few things first...

buy new snugglies at Kohl's,
hit the winery,
spend the entire day
on the beach at Rocky Neck,
and come Monday morning,
get to work on this thing.

Your legs bounced rapid fire on the floor.
Your eyes were far away.
You were planning your attack.

The Heathen

Even as I have seen, they that plow iniquity, and sow wickedness, reap the same.
~ Job 4:8
(For my father)

Mother has been harvesting –
wat a liiv an bambaie –
for a year now, throwing away all your things.

She placed your jewelry in a wooden box
lined with fake blue velvet;
six American flag tie-tacks,
two bi-plane tie-clasps,
and crossed fork and knife cuff-links.
There were six watches,
each one holding fast to a single moment,
and there were political buttons –
I Like Ike,
Wallace for President,
and a white button with the image
of an assault rifle and the words,
Come And Take It.

She passed the box around;
whatever we wouldn't take
she tossed.

I took the fork and knife cufflinks.

She also chucked out your clothes –
your pants, gold yellow, sunglow yellow, Mikado yellow,
asparagus green, lawn and lime green,
and your belts,
a white vinyl belt,

a belt with a big J.S. buckle,
an American flag buckle,
gun buckles,
and all your socks –

nylon, knee-high, and black –
except the brand new ones,
which she gave to “the poor,”
and your sweaters,
v-neck, scoop neck,
cowl neck, turtleneck, crew neck,
cable knit and cardigan, and collared shirts –
a shirt without a collar is *not* a shirt;
it’s underwear.

She would not live with them,
she would not put up with them another day,
these abandoned refugees,
emaciated infidels,
lounging around day after day,
doing absolutely nothing
since you’ve been gone.

Exodus

And Moses stretched out his hand over the sea; and the Lord caused the sea to go back... and the waters were divided.
~ Exodus 14:21-22

The leaves begin to flag, wearied by summer,
their green silks wilting; their will to hang on 'til
the Joe Pye Weed has passed, has withered too.

The air is full of hummingbirds, ticking and thrumming,
vibrating wards of anything remotely red,
which the entire landscape will be soon enough,

and goldfinches disappear within the primrose,
the perfect camouflage before they burst,
per-chik-a-ree, a handful of tossed yellow,

and way out in the distance the Juncos surge
past the millions of red-winged blackbirds, grackles,
cowbirds, and starlings; they are powering south,

but the Juncos follow the snow, as here the landscape,
with all its tiny life that stays behind,
readies its gray rags to hunker down.

From the back deck I watch the exodus,
as a heavy eastern wind parts the warmth,
walls of waning color on either side,

the cold coming in, a frigid white horse.

Jammin'

Bushnell Audtorium
Hartford, Connecticut
June 22, 1975

Before I knew a thing about a thing,
intuition had purchased Bob's *Burnin'*
from the cut-out bin at Spag's in Worcester, Mass.,
and a few months later I spotted a tiny ad –
Coming to the Bushnell – Bob Morley and the Whalers –
and there I was among the few down front,
the rest of the cavernous hall completely empty.

Bob was recently risen from the smoke
of civil war that battered the streets of Trenchtown.
This was June of 1975,
a year and a half before *Smile Jamaica,*
which no one could have dreamt. But what I knew
was that on the back of *Burnin'* Nesta held
a massive spliff fatter than his fingers,
and the lilt of patois floated in the air
there in the Bushnell on that summer night.

As Bob recalled observing the hypocrites
the strap on his guitar had come undone
and fallen to the stage; while both his hands
covered up his eyes he sang a promise –
Every likkle ting gone be all right!
But soon enough he'd learn that wasn't true.

A roadie rushed on stage and lifted the guitar,
as Bob, a Rasta dervish, jogged in place.
He reached around Bob's body and strapped it on,
as Nesta chanted of Georgie's fire light.

This was June of 1975,
the Wailers dressed in uniforms of brutality
for reasons it would take me years to grasp.

Smile Jamaica Concert
National Heroes Park in Kingston, Jamaica
December 5, 1976

Michael Manley invited Bob to write
a song that would lift Jamaicans above the din
of war, but people felt that this was a sign
that Bob endorsed the PNP, and so
threats of death began to roam the streets.

The tune that Bob would pen was *Smile Jamaica*;
he'd uplift his Idren with a tender cry –
Oh lord, help us tonight. Cast away the evil
spell, throw some water in the well,
and smile in Jamaica.

But by December
third of '76 there were the signs
of the violence that would soon descend on Bob.

From 56 Hope Road Bob would emerge
between two cops, his bloody shirt an emblem
of the war that raged on Trenchtown's narrow streets.
And two days later Bob would do the show,
agreeing to come and only do *one song*
for the thousands in attendance that December night.

When someone asked him why he'd take this risk,
he said, *The people who are trying to make this world*
worse aren't taking a day off. How can I?

And the one song he would sing became a full
90-minute performance in the face of death.

The air was smoke, the stage a small black space
where people loitered close around Tuff Gong.
What could he be thinking in the cathedral of
his wounded consciousness that we could not,
in 400 years, ever begin to imagine,
under those flashing, fabricated bolts of lightning?

I wonder stupidly if I could roll
my left sleeve up and show the marks of teeth,
bare my chest to say that I'm right here
standing at the center of confrontation
chanting Selassie I in the face of danger,
chanting the one song that was agreed upon..
...until the basic human rights are equally
guaranteed to all, without regard to race –
dis a war...and we know we shall win...

... though, of course, it couldn't be a single song.
Bob had more to say, and so he did.
Get up! Stand up! Chase those crazy baldheads
Out of our town! Cast away that spell!
Political violence will fill your city, yeah!
There I vision through the seas of oppression
that, my Lord, they're coming after me.
They stab you in the back, and they claim
that you're not looking. Dance to Jah music...
Is a foolish dog bark at a flying bird.
Say one bright morning when my work is over,
Man will fly away home... Mr. Cop,
Hey, Mr. Cop, ain't got no... hey Mr. Cop...
Inite oneself and love Imanity!

One Love Peace Concert
The National Stadium in Kingston, Jamaica
April 22, 1978

The Bushnell seated nearly 4,000,
but on June 22 in 1975
a couple of hundred people sat down front.

How different things would be in '76
on the grounds of the National Stadium in Jamaica.

The gates opened up at 2 o'clock;
the show was set to start at 5:00 p.m.
The crown prince of Ethiopia
sited up the concert organizers'
vision and commitment for a peace.
Then The Meditations rocked at five.
Althea and Donna brought *Uptown Top Ranking –*
Gimme likkle bass… me wine up me waist.
Then came Oku Onoura, guerilla from
up in the hills, his writing declared subversive,
and confiscated when he was in jail.
As the audience grew, Oku chant *Dread Times.*
Then Junior Tucker, Jamaica's Michael Jackson,
and Culture and a youthful Dennis Brown.
Trinity followed by the Mighty Diamonds.
Leroy Smart, Inner Circle with Jacob,
then Big Youth big up with a line of hits,
and as Manley and Seaga took their seats,
Beres Hammond and Zap Pow come with it.
The leaders' wives, and members of parliament,
the diplomatic corps, the police commissioner,
the Jamaica Defence Force chief of staff all seated.
Photographers and members of the press,

journalists, both local and worldwide,
all were seated when Peter Tosh came out
detonating message after message,
brandishing his locks and a massive spliff.
Ras Michael and the Sons of Negus drummed
and chanted as anticipation grew.
The alarm was sounded when The Wailers hit
the stage to a deafening applause,
as in the blaze of one dazzling spotlight
Bob appeared against the mammoth backdrop
of the Lion of Judah, and the I-Threes sang,
… *if you listen carefully now you will hear…*

There were stormy skies that night and lightning flashed,
and thunder rumbled over a whirling Bob,
a reeling Bob, his dreams of hope coursing
through his body and tossing him around,
an exquisite twirling jam in the name of the Lord.

Well, I'm trying to say, could we have, could
we have, up here on stage here the presence
of Mr. Michael Manley and Mr. Edward
Seaga. I just want to shake hands and show
the people that we're gonna make it right…

Seaga showed up first, then Manley came,
and Bob embraced them both and hopped in place,
ignited by the light of Jah, his face
ecstatic as he held their hands; he couldn't
see their deadpan faces or what was lurking
in the battered, broken war zones of their hearts,
though he knew, and still he held their hands
above his head, and folded their fingers together
and chanted love, prosperity, and Jah!

Below the deafening applause Manley clapped,
and Seaga seemed to just look straight ahead,
as the people on the stage were filled with joy
for a moment. But soon the stadium was empty,
the thunder had the evening to itself,
the lightning flashed upon a barren field,
and the crowd dispersed to their respective wars.

And so there it was. The leaders of
this most famous, despairing call for peace
were gone.

But nothing changed. In 1980
another ruthless war between the usual
factions. And the number of Jamaicans killed?
The count for this election was 800;
800 Jamaicans killed.

And it wasn't until
May 21 of 1981,
just 10 days after Bob would leave this world,
that they would face each other once again,
Manley and Seaga, and extend
their hands to one another as they had
three years before on stage, as Bob proclaimed,
holding their hands in the air above his head,
the spirit of God, Jah! Rastafari!

Waiting In Vain

And now, Lord, for what do I wait? My hope is in You.
~ Psalms 39:7

January 26, 1957
The Connecticut Sportsmen's and Boat Show
Hartford Armory, Hartford, Connecticut

I once read that actor George Bessolo,
AKA George Reeves, while playing the
mild mannered reporter Clark Kent,

found that the pressure of acting the incompetent
and keeping hidden that incredibly weighty secret
was his biggest challenge; not *getting the story*
or *meeting the deadline*, but keeping Superman
as far away from Kent as possible.

I didn't know from George Bessolo,
or George Reeves. I was utterly consumed
with wonder; would Superman fly just once
up near the roof of the big gymnasium?
I must have asked my father what he thought
a thousand times that chilly afternoon
as we drove across the Bulkeley Bridge.
I can see him now, big leather-gloved hands
around the turquoise steering wheel of the Plymouth
station wagon, baby blue, and standard
on the column, with WTIC
on the radio, and his Russian hat of fur
with earflaps so big you'd think that *he* could fly.

We were headed for the sportsmen's show,
billed as the single greatest "Sports Show" on Earth,
and were on our way to witness a miracle,
not Dale Long or Johnny Kucks, or Maglie,
not Don Newcombe or even Yogi Berra.
We weren't going to see the *tank show thrillers,*
nor were we going to fish for trophy trout
in the Berkshire Trout Farm Pool, stocked to the hilt.
Admission was a dollar fourteen cents,
sixty cents if you were just a kid.
All it would take was 60¢ for me
to stand inside a building where Superman
would shake my hand then fly around the room.

The Hartford Armory gym was packed and bustling,
though I can't recall a single face amid
the swarm of puffer jackets trimmed with orange,
crowded in and leaning around the tanks
to watch the rolling logs, the racing tubs,
the *thrilling shows* unfolding before their eyes.

I never spoke a word, but followed my dad
to stand in line and wait for the sensation.
There was no seeing above or around this mob,
but I was so immersed in imagination,
in the colors and sounds and actions in my mind,
that whatever stood before me was only myth.
The truth, however, was that I would soon
be standing face-to-face with Superman,
letting him know in my own covert way
that his secret was safe with me, and that he could
trust me implicitly. And when it was
our turn, he shook my hand in silence as

he looked across the wide gymnasium,
maybe at Jimmy Geataniello's trout,
a 2 pound rainbow, the biggest of the show.
I didn't speak and neither did Clark Kent.
And that was it.

Later in the car,
I worked very hard to deflect the fact
that Superman was smaller than my dad,
that his suit was wrinkled and didn't fit too well,
and that he hadn't flown around the gym at all.

That was the day that Superman became
a member of The Corps of Disappointment
inhabited by the likes of Santa Claus,
the fairy that swipes your tooth and leaves you cash,
the giant rabbit that leaves you chicken eggs,
the Sandman, sprinkling grains of sand into
your eyes to make your dreams more magical.

And yet for years I told myself that he
hadn't flown around that gym because
the room was just too small for him to manage;
I knew the truth but was clutching at the lore.
I knew better than to think that George
might have flown above the hunters there,
or that the bullet would bang against his skull
and simply fall to the floor at his stocking feet,
George Bessolo, sitting on the edge of a bed,
smiling strangely and staring into the dark,
a spent shell casing glinting on the rug.

Turn Your Lights Down Low

But in those days, after that tribulation, the sun shall be darkened,
and the moon shall not give her light...
~ Mark 13:24

His rage is the sound of furniture being broken,
of shattering glass and small things angrily thrown –
a pen, an empty beer can, or some words
hurtling out, the shrapnel from the bomb
of his sadness exploding over and over.

But you mustn't think of him as someone who's
one dimensional, a bitter man.
His humor, equally sharp and quick, includes
a spot-on take on Rodney Dangerfield,
but with jokes that he has made himself,
sardonic little ditties that he tells
in a way that lets us know that he's aware
that his is a planet much too far to reach.

These are the two extremes he's able to show;
the rest of what he is remains unseen,
the dark side of this man, a captive of
the music that he knows but will not play,
his roiling lack of patience for the world.

But that's a sham too. Everyone knows
his dark side isn't really dark at all;
it's just that we can't see and so we say
that there's a lack of inspiration there,
no burning lights of compulsive motivation,
but vague mysteries that we must surmise
are ambiguities that we decide are *truth.*

He sits alone on the rocks along the beach,
the spring tide reaching up below the moon
which spends her days on the task of gathering in
and letting out her wet and massive blankets,
taking away and giving back at once.

He heeds the lesson here, his isolation
calling us in to try to comprehend,
pushing us away with tidal slowness,
this *mast* intoxicated by his thoughts
of that far-off night horizon all lit up,
the lamps of every single room ablaze,
the doors of all the entryways locked shut.

Three Little Birds

Look at the birds of the air, for they neither sow nor reap nor gather into barns;
yet your heavenly Father feeds them.
~ Matthew 6:26-34

father

A late October afternoon
in sepia damp Dennisport,
on the beachfront deck
of a salty stale motel,
three sparrows
on three beach rose boughs
an arm's length away,
the frail sparseness of tarnished branches
and the withered, coppery flowers
against the backdrop of sand,
and sand-colored sea,
each branch, each bird
symmetrical in the tangle
of sedge and wind,
as if they have escaped
by necessity,
an overcrowded nest,
fled the keening traffic
and dismal cul-de-sacs,
and landed here,
this trinity of sparrows,
the two outer birds
looking in at the center bird
as if he were The Father.

son

November's smoke swells on the horizon.
The wind mimics the sea,
and what flutters in the battered maple
are butterflies of leaves
rusted and dying down
against late October's craggy scrim.
Pluviophile in withdrawal,
swallowing the wind,
hoping to taste rain
and the memory of a day
from childhood,
alone and terrified,
when the sky was heavy gray,
wave- clouds moving
above the desolate trees,
and rain approaching
with a cure.

holy ghost

The place named for the distance
between the center of Kingston
and a little house in the hills
where the first steps were taken
of an improbable saga,
and a small rock
became a metaphor
for a larger rock,
one I'd stand on for a moment,
looking this way
down the immigrant avenue

of wooden four-story walk-ups,
and that way

into the verdant hills
under rags of heat
that could not be shed.

When I walked the icy sidewalk
of my youth
I'd whisper,
Step on a crack
break your mother's back,
as luxuriant forests flourished
outside my doorstep,
in the hills of imagination
where a short stretch of road
reached into the future
asking nothing of anyone.

One Love/People Get Ready

And I will give them one heart, and one way, that they may fear me forever, for the good of them, and of their children after them.
~ Jeremiah 32:39
(Homage to Dennis Brutus)

one love

There's no art – this much I understand –
to find the mind's construction in the face,
and I'd surmise yours had to be unreadable
as you'd look into the sky from your cell.

Was that mortal light the light of vision,
the invisible line that tethered you to truth,
the first light and the last light intertwined,
the light of one love many millennia old?

When, from your solitary cell, you'd lean
toward the evening sky when it was clear,
you'd sometimes manage to see a single star,
the anticipated inspiration, the show,

the furtive rendezvous with the voiceless muse.
That solitary star became the theater,
the light that shone at the end of the proverbial tunnel,
the period that lit the end of an unwritten poem.

people get ready

Your falling hammers punctuated stones,
you and Nelson, Zuma and Kgalema.
Could you have ever imagined Robben Island
as a tourist attraction, former prisoners as guards,

pointing out the beauty of the penguins
and the seals, calling your attention
to Minto Hill with its ghosts of fires that warned
of rocks that would devour wayward ships.

And would you speak of lepers arriving from
heaven and from hell, and would you tell
of Moturu Kramat, that place where saying farewell
was a sacred act. And all along the way

would you stop to let more passengers embark,
the old train grinding away toward a new land,
chuffing toward some light through *the rains of poison*?

NOTES

Page 17, "I Shot the Sheriff" – the lines *"... and the moon is out,/ a little hole too small to push your head through..."* is an allusion to Elizabeth Bishop's poem "The Man-Moth."

Page 26, "Small Axe" – The form here resembles a renga, a Japanese form that began over seven hundred years ago to inspire the collaborative composition of poems. Normally poets worked in pairs or small groups, taking turns composing the alternating three-line and two-line stanzas; of course, in this case, I wrote the poem alone. Linked together, renga were often hundreds of lines long. To create a renga, one poet writes the first stanza, a haiku. The next poet adds the second stanza, a couplet with seven syllables per line. Re: the reference to McCain – when my father's Alzheimer's was really ramping up he became fixated on John McCain, believing that McCain had been a World War II hero, and a member of his – my father's generation.

Page 33, "Duppy Conquerer" – *Duppy* is a Jamaican Patois word of Northwest African origin meaning ghost or spirit. Much of Caribbean folklore revolves around duppies. Duppies are often regarded as malevolent spirits.

Page 37, "Rastaman Chant" – *thunder, funde, akete* – Nyabinghi drumming is performed as a communal meditative practice. Three kinds of drums (called"harps") are used in Nyabinghi: the *thunder*, also known as the "Pope Smasher" or "Vatican Basher," strikes loudly on the first beat, and softly on the third beat (of four). The middle-pitched *akete* (also known as the "repeater") plays an improvised syncopation. The *funde* plays a regular one-two beat. The other drums keep regular rhythms while the *akete* players solo in a kind of conversation.

Page 47, "So Much Things to Say" – George Tyler – On October 14, 1910, Marcus Garvey received a visit in his Harlem office from George Tyler, who pulled a .38-caliber revolver and fired four shots, wounding Garvey in the right leg and scalp. Tyler was captured and arrested. He committed suicide by leaping from the third tier of the Harlem jail as he was being taken to his arraignment.

Paul Bogle was a Jamaican Baptist deacon and is a National Hero of Jamaica. He was a leader of the 1865 Morant Bay Protesters, who agitated for justice and fair treatment for all people in Jamaica. After leading the Morant Bay rebellion, Bogle was captured by British authorities and hanged on October 24, 1865 in the Morant Bay Court House.

Page 48, "So Much Things to Say" – the word *ignorancy* is used occasionally in reggae music instead of *ignorance.* You also sometimes see *violency* instead of *violence.*

Page 54, "Jammin'" – Bob Marley and the Wailers played at the Bushnell Auditorium on June 22, 1975 to a crowd of only a few hundred. His appearance was not well advertised. In fact, an ad in tiny print in a local paper read – *Coming to the Bushnell – Bob Morley and the Whalers.*

Page 56 – *Tuff Gong* is one of Bob Marley's nicknames, and echoes of one of the nicknames given to Leonard "The Gong" Howell, one of the founders of Rastafari.

Page 64, "Turn Your Lights Down Low" – In Sufi philosophy, a *mast* (pronounced "must") is a person who is overwhelmed with love for God, accompanied with external disorientation resembling intoxication. The word is coined by Meher Baba and originates from the Sufi term *mast-Allah* meaning "intoxicated with God."

Page 68, "One Love/People Get Ready" – Dennis Brutus was a South African activist, educator, journalist, and poet best known for his campaign to have apartheid South Africa banned from the Olympic Games.

Page 69 – *The rains of poison* is from Dennis Brutus' poem, *Longing.*

About the Author

John L. Stanizzi is the author of the chapbook *Windows*. His full length collections are *Ecstasy Among Ghosts*, *Sleepwalking*, *Dance Against the Wall*, and *After the Bell*. His poems have appeared in *Prairie Schooner*, *The New York Quarterly*, *Tar River Poetry*, *Rattle*, *Passages North*, *The Spoon River Quarterly*, *Poet Lore*, *The Connecticut River Review*, *Freshwater*, and many other publications. Twice nominated for the Pushcart Prize, in 1998 Stanizzi was named The New England Poet of the Year by The New England Association of Teachers of English. John has been a judge for the Connecticut Poetry Out Loud Program, the 2011 Connecticut Book Award for Poetry, and the Sunken Garden Poetry Award for Adult Writers. He is the coordinator for Hill-Stead Museum's Fresh Voices Poetry Competition for high school poets. He taught for many years at Bacon Academy where he also directed the theater program. He has read at many venues throughout Connecticut, including The Sunken Garden Poetry Festival, RJ Julia Booksellers, and the Arts Café Mystic. He is currently an adjunct professor at Manchester Community College. He lives with his wife, Carol, in Coventry, Connecticut. Visit him at www.johnlstanizzi.com

11169905R00045

Printed in Great Britain
by Amazon.co.uk, Ltd.,
Marston Gate.